200 Creative Writing Prompts Workbook

Story Starters
for Journals
and
Inspiration to Overcome
Writer's Block

Compiled by
Debra Chapoton, author

ISBN: 9798672666204
Imprint: Independently published

Books by Debra Chapoton

EDGE OF ESCAPE
SHELTERED
THE GUARDIAN'S DIARY
EXODIA
OUT OF EXODIA
A SOUL'S KISS
THE GIRL IN THE TIME MACHINE
TO DIE UPON A KISS
THE TIME BENDER
THE TIME PACER
THE TIME STOPPER
THE TIME ENDER
HERE WITHOUT A TRACE
BRAIN POWER PUZZLES series
HOW TO TEACH A FOREIGN LANGUAGE
HOW TO HELP YOUR CHILD SUCCEED IN SCHOOL
HOW TO BLEND FAMILIES
CROSSING THE SCRIPTURES
300 TEACHER HACKS AND TIPS
THE SECRET IN THE HIDDEN CAVE
MYSTERY'S GRAVE
BULLIES AND BEARS
BIGFOOT DAY, NINJA NIGHT
A TICK IN TIME
THE TUNNEL series
and more
Visit bigpinelodgebooks.com

Foreword:

When readers care deeply about your characters, your setting, and your plot they can lose themselves completely in your writing. But remember, story magic doesn't happen by accident. You have to work at it.

Here are two hundred story prompts to get you started writing. Be creative. Imagine a story around the phrases you're given. Don't write it down. Then imagine another, something completely different, and write that one down. Try to outdo your first attempt. Don't overdo it. Edit, trim it down, read it aloud. Try to appeal to one sense in each short scene. Don't overload with sights, smells, sounds, feels and feelings, but do include at least one of these.

Good writing often comes after much daydreaming. Authors create in their heads, listening to the voices there, carrying on conversations, plotting out stories and scenes endlessly, and then they write down the best, unforgettable ones.

Have fun with this. If something doesn't inspire you right away, try changing a word. The prompt doesn't have to be the first sentence; it can come in the middle or be the ending.

On the following pages you will find 200 writing prompts. Read one and let your imagination run. Who's in this scene? What just happened? What's about to happen? Start writing.

Sample (with self-edits):
Prompt: It was just a grizzled old guy, shuffling in to buy a pack of cigarettes.

Tory turned away. ~~You~~ She couldn't be too careful, even an old ~~guy~~ dude could be the one to catch her. She rounded the corner and ~~looked at~~ browsed the selection in the candy aisle. The door chimed again. She peeked ~~through~~ above the peppermint patties, wishing she could ~~just~~ go home. ~~Maybe~~ Absently she tore open the wrapper, took a bite and watched another teen, as ragged as she, enter.
"Want me to pay for that?" the old man asked, his lips curling up in an uncomfortable smile. He had come around the corner as a cop … or a pervert.

For those of you using these prompts **to break writer's block**, find a prompt and rework it to fit where you are in your manuscript. For example, the above prompt could be inspiration to write something like this:

His boss, a grizzled old geezer always reeking of smoke, shuffled past him and winked.

1. Her ragged skirt and socks were more woven of mud than cotton

2. "Dude, nobody does that out here."

3. A stream of molten gold was what I saw first.

4. Hungry, hungry for flesh and blood and muscle, but …

5. Her throat swelled; her eyes closed with unshed tears as she …

6. "Hey, not there."

7. Her eyes roam back to the lamps, standing like guards …

8. When the tragedy happened, they were, of course, together.

9. Slightly larger than a European principality, the parking lot was now full of …

10. She'd want to hold his face in her hands and tell him …

11. A few self-pitying drops traced down her nose when he …

____

____

____

____

____

____

____

12. He paused as a hundred thoughts swooped through his head.

____

____

____

____

____

____

____

13. Sacks of soil slouched among them like …

14. "No, of course not, I'd never do that."

15. Work three of these verbs into a scene: howl, moan, creak, clap, slosh, entangle, pare, squawk, spun, bleed, detonate, drift, chomp, snarl, hiss, trample, shimmy, gush.

____

____

____

____

____

____

____

16. Use 3 more of the above verbs.

____

____

____

____

____

____

____

17. Those twin ribbons of steel looked like …

18. Someone in back stage whispered the truth: "He's blind."

19. A decal on each of the Plexiglas windows warned …

____

____

____

____

____

____

____

20. He concentrated on being patient. This would take …

____

____

____

____

____

____

____

21. Her shoulders strained with the weight of …

22. "No, not again. What else did he say?"

23. There were waterfalls of stairs beneath the windows …

24. You name it and it's there. Like …

25. The wind-whipped snow meant …

____

____

____

____

____

____

____

26. It was cool in some ways and dangerous in others.

____

____

____

____

____

____

____

27. The concrete walls exuded a damp lime smell at that depth.

28. "Brats. That's what they are." She flicked her ash out the window.

29. That woman was a disciplined tornado.

30. "Selfish? Me? Just what are you really saying?"

31. Blearily, she glimpsed black clothing, a white face, and

32. The voices in her head said something different entirely.

33. A stunning amber sunset beyond a chaotic mass of building tops could not be ignored.

34. I wondered how long they would float.

35. The breeze carried the subtle scent of flowers she did not recognize.

36. Rufus looked down his nose at the ruffian and said, "…

37. The thing billowed over the grass causing it to move in waves like an ocean.

____

____

____

____

____

____

____

38. I had no idea he was about to …

____

____

____

____

____

____

____

39. The distant sound of a latch being drawn disturbed the peace and quiet.

40. Shame enveloped her. How could she have done that?

41. The class was full, every seat taken, but I …

42. Snapping peas and picking cucumbers with my grandmother meant all was right with the world. That summer …

43. One sock had stayed up to her knee, but the other had given up ages ago and flopped limply around her ankle.

44. Her hair was interspersed with braids, tied at the ends with bits of chicken wire.

45. Strands of long white hair had run for freedom from her bun and languished in draggles around her shoulders.

46. He felt orphaned, abandoned.

47. His old, old hands were gnarled and wrinkled like the bark of an oak.

48. What wouldn't he do to see her again? He suddenly knew what he would do.

49. She gasped in each breath, tears streaming from her eyes.

____

____

____

____

____

____

____

50. And that was the sweetest thing I ever did for someone.

____

____

____

____

____

____

____

51. There was a strange humming howl coming from the space ship and the hairs on her arms rose as the air became charged.

52. The eggs hatched, the seeds should have been planted, but …

53. With a face-splitting yawn, he …

54. He answered a few more questions about China before class ended.

55. What you need to do is lock this thing in and throw away the key.

56. The ends were held tight with blue gummers.

57. What I wore on my feet were for styling, not striding—shoes that would make a preacher covetous.

58. "She's not ready," I yelled. Then, less hysterically, I repeated, "She's just not ready."

59. Celina had on glorified nurse's shoes, ugly as newborn puppies, but a plus in a street race.

60. "Follow the clues," he said. So I did.

61. From a hundred feet away, I can tell that she is not herself.

62. During the pandemic I couldn't see mom. She turned 101 alone.

63. The kitchen is outfitted with paring knives, boning knives, carving knives, and cleavers.

64. "Who on earth knows what that little thingy opens?"

65. Her voice was that of a woman who has breathed the dust of a thousand roads.

66. She gave him a smile and a nod toward the entryway.

67. The cougar slowly advanced upon the second goose, waiting for his prey to look him in the eye.

____

____

____

____

____

____

____

68. "There's always something wrong, isn't there?"

____

____

____

____

____

____

____

____

69. He had no choice but to fidget.

70. This was, and forever would be, the worst day of his life.

71. Uncle Sammy had the same white hair and weary professionalism as …

72. A few moments later they met in the dining hall and laughed at their respective costumes.

73. In front of them, a Formica coffee table was littered with magazines.

74. Will held tightly onto Kimmy's arm and swiped at the giant webs with his torch.

75. Though old she still held remnants of pretty.

76. His legs gave way and he slumped down.

77. Jennie was the only child to inherit the olive skin tone and dark hair from …

78. He poked the body with the bloodied end of his sword.

79. He watches every move as if he knows my heart is pounding away.

80. Danny mulled over the unexpected information.

81. He shifted his muscular frame.

82. Leave me alone, I thought, but out loud I said, …

83. "Yeah, we will," Bob said, and she was surprised by his insinuating tone.

____

____

____

____

____

____

____

84. The twins negated the suggestion with synchronous head shake.

____

____

____

____

____

____

____

85. "So they're not allowed to make any announcements material to the ..." His mind had begun to wander.

86. Liam shook his head almost imperceptibly, but his father noticed and gave him a smack.

87. She heard the thump. Chills up her spine followed.

____

____

____

____

____

____

____

88. The detective discovered the scuffed tracks beside the dilapidated barn.

____

____

____

____

____

____

89. Olivia was one of those women who dresses against her beauty.

90. Will could read his face and knew that he'd soon pay the price.

91. Max was a dark complected man in his mid-forties wearing a crisp green collared shirt and black-framed glasses.

92. The secretary got them settled in plastic seats facing the desk.

93. **Use five of these Adjectives in a scene:** gnarled, rotted, bloated, discarded, trampled, threadbare, barebones, far-flung, spent, ghastly, baleful, opulent, frothy, surefooted

94. Use five more of the above adjectives in the same scene from a different perspective.

95. Sheilah moved about the bank with such ponderous dignity that to a child she appeared to be …

96. The woman shifted her gaze to Ling Wong who immediately lowered her eyes.

97. She had studied hard, and now it all came naturally to her.

98. Jojo spied the ATV idling in the grass, a loaded wagon attached.

99. What she noticed first were the scarred rock walls.

100. The sounds and smells of traffic welcomed them to civilization.

101. Winter howled across the plains and stripped it bare.

102. A twinge of suspicion had begun to grow since docking the boat.

103. A sinuous voice lured her in.

104. Spray-soaked stones carpeted the path.

105. The air quickened.

____

____

____

____

____

____

____

106. The moon threw its shadow to the earth.

____

____

____

____

____

____

____

107. Shadows moved like dreams across the silk curtains.

108. She hid under an avalanche of lace.

109. A chaotic tussle ensued.

110. Banners coiled like black flame.

111. The exhausted farmer carried groaning buckets of fruit.

112. Finally, a door slammed open, and a thick shaft of light entered the room.

113. "Welcome to America," a bespectacled official announced.

114. The outside lamp buzzed. A cloud of flies began to swarm them.

115. Mothers held listless infants in their arms while their older, hollow-eyed children clung to their skirts.

____

116. Some silent signal finally reached the attendant, and he motioned for us to climb the ladder and board the boat.

117. They were brimming with health.

118. Each sound that reached him was like a symphony, each sight a painting, each breath a sip of wine.

119. "I've no qualifications as a flirt. You mustn't make fun of me."

120. He gripped the armrest of the chair as his breaths grew ragged.

121. A small flickering flame rose from the lamp, blackened the glass, then went out.

122. He took off his hat to wipe sweat from his forehead, revealing close-cropped, light blond hair.

123. He was an attractive man, she thought, the muscles of her jaw clenching and unclenching as she stood there.

124. Charlie wore dirty jeans, a colorful short-sleeved shirt, and a stained wide-brimmed hat.

125. The glittering carapace protected everything vulnerable underneath.

______

126. We needed first names that were elegant, names that gave us confidence or that had pizzazz.

______

127. Her spine was curled like a shrimp's, her skin as mottled as camouflage.

128. I experienced a kaleidoscope of color and glittering smiles, seeming to move me into infinity.

129. The music allowed me inside itself, immersed in a space where time didn't exist.

130. My stomach felt strangely empty. It was as if I'd been hollowed out by that wave.

131. He smiled, his teeth gray in the dark.

132. We paused in the doorway, wanting to blurt the truth, but afraid of how he'd react.

133. Change was going to come; I felt its hot breath draw near.

134. It shriveled up like an old raisin and rolled away.

135. I was struck by the gunmetal gray light of sundown.

136. The sky looked gray and bruised.

137. Granny sat wedged into the passenger seat like a watermelon in a sock.

138. They all stood there watching her as the chill wind pummeled them.

139. The crash knocked his helmet from his head and tossed him down three feet away, unconscious and, though no one knew it at the time, dying.

140. Trust is everything. The instant the words were out of her mouth she remembered the last time she'd said them.

141. It had been a cool, steely day in the season that passed for winter.

142. I coasted through a haze of fog.

143. Words were lost in the crunching sound of ...

144. He was just flirting, casting the kind of line that only men like him could handle.

145. His gift had the appearance of sincerity and depth.

146. Tim and Andy merged into the traffic of adulthood.

147. They claimed he could see a way through any emotional conflict, but …

148. More often than not, she'd mentioned the purity of his heart.

149. They had bloomed early this year, as they always did after a mild winter. In another two weeks there would be saucer-size blossoms.

150. We walk through snow that comes up to our knees.

151. I remember having the strangest feeling that I could see our words; they seemed to be written in the steam of our breath.

152. Watery gray skies melted into the sea, the line between them a smudge of coal.

153, The clouds were slim and spread out beneath a pale cerulean sky.

154. Those same clouds could suddenly bunch together like school-yard bullies, releasing a torrent of rain so vicious that …

155. A few rays of bright sunlight fell like gold through the heavy, moss-draped branches.

156. Memories sifted through the air, falling like rain to the ground around them.

157. Did I even have dreams at that tender age?

158. He backed up a step, keeping as much floor as possible between them.

159. Then she smiled and pushed to her feet, her knees popping and cracking at the suddenness of her movement.

160. Evil, he was, now listening to the slow evening-out of the girl's breathing.

161. She was a girl who knew that life was unfair and love could break your heart.

162. Pudgy pink hands glided across the table top, searching for crumbs.

163. His knees felt weak, and fear was a cold knot in his stomach.

164. He hung onto his world by a fraying thread.

165. I could still smell the cellar's moist, moldy air, feel its chill touching my face and arms.

166. The air felt heavy, electric.

167. I wonder if this could actually be a form of magic, changing us until we saw our souls.

168. I imagined them at opposite sides of the room, she all smiles, he with his arms crossed, defiant.

169.He examined me, eyes dark blue and hostile.

170. The terror that had been gripping the nape of my neck had loosened.

171. The tea was lapsang souchong, dark amber with smoky depths.

172. These are the small sparks of joy in my dreary existence.

173. "I'm not hungry," I lied, even as my stomach rumbled a low, disloyal growl.

174. It felt like the unrelenting throb of a toothache.

175. The polished floorboards gleamed like honey but the empty attic rooms couldn't shake their forlorn air.

176. The wall peeled its faded paper; the window gaped naked.

177. Old clothes spilled from gaping boxes, magazines and newspapers slid into heaps, stacks of broken furniture threatened to topple and crush us.

178. It was just a grizzled old guy, shuffling in to buy a pack of cigarettes.

179. Inside, the living room dimmed before my sun-dazzled eyes.

180. I listened to the tick of the clock and breathed in the smells of smoke and lemon oil soap.

181. I leafed through the pages, breathing in the musty smell of unaired paper.

182. He had sharp features and a hooded gaze.

183. He had terrified me as a child, with his ability to …

184. Was that how it began? With a look, a brush of my hair, a touch?

185. When we were alone, he …

186. His lips touched mine, his cheeks rough on my face, the warmth of his body against my own.

187. A few seconds later, they were gone, leaving me alone in the half-lit cellar.

188. My questions hovered like stirred dust and then settled down again, unanswered.

189. But then she heaved a little sigh that was almost undetectable.

190. I broke it off over a phone call, a crystal-clear, long-distance conversation.

191. Because I wasn't brave enough to see his face, I lost the only thing that ever …

192. The large gaps between the trees allowed for easy passage.

193. There was no path this far from civilization.

194. She stifled a squeak as thorns scraped her arms.

195. Her feet slapped the beats of freedom into the cold damp sand.

196. The wind lifted her hair; the smell of sea salt flared her nostrils as the waves in the distance crashed.

197. Something loped by on wide paws beneath a body of pale fur.

198. The smell of pine trees was the sweet scent of memories—freedom, he thought, and home.

199. Services have been held here without a roof ever since the hurricane.

200. There was something in the air, something that …

www.ingramcontent.com/pod-product-compliance
Lightning Source LLC
Chambersburg PA
CBHW081235250726
48654CB00012B/1338